To . . . .

From . . . .

the delinquent fairy's thoughts on
feng shui

lauren white

SOURCEBOOKS, INC.®
NAPERVILLE, ILLINOIS

HeLLo, My nAMe is FIo, aNd dEspiTe beiNg a FAiry, I, like MosT pEopLe, am seArcHiNg FoR PeAce aNd HapPiness in My Life...

UnFoRTUNaTely, theRE's no mAgic foRMULa (otherwise I'd USE it!)...

BUT LIVING BY THE PRINCIPLES OF FENG SHUI HELPS. BASICALLY, FENG SHUI (PRONOUNCED FOONG SHWAY) is tHE ANCIENT CHINESE SYSTEM OF hARNESSING THE dyNAMIC FLOW OF ENERGY,

dyNAMIC FLOW OF ENERGY — CALLED "Chi".

to AChIEVE HARMONY AND BALANCE...

(Flo in Harmony with nature!)

Using things like water, plants, windchimes, and rearranging your furniture according to the

PRINCIPLES OF FENG SHUI CAN
PROMOTE PEACE AND WELL-being.
THE WORDS ACTUALLY MEAN
"WIND" AND "WATER," AND
bALANCING THESE FORCES CAN
bRING INCREDIBLE reSULTS.

(tHE FENG SHUI MASTER!)

FOR EXAMPLE, YOUR WEALTH CORNER IS IN THE SOUTHEAST. IF YOU PLACE A LEAFY PLANT IN THIS CORNER OF YOUR LIVING ROOM, IT WILL INCREASE YOUR PROSPERITY . . .

THIS bOOK GiVES yoU tHE lowdowN, "Flo-STyle," on aLL THE bASiCS aNd How To acHiEvE Life-loNg HappiNESS aNd good foRtUNE — (weLL, SORT of ...)

FENG SHUi :0

MAKE suRE yoU'RE NevER witHoUT yoUR FeNg SHUi bOOk, yoU NeVer KNow wHEN iT WiLL COME iN hANdy...

KEEP YOUR CHI IN CHECK . . .

..... there is good Chi...

... and there is bad Chi......

mirrors reflect

everything !!!

TEAM WORK !

SNAKE: STABILITY, decision-mak

In FENG SHUi, aNiMaLS REPRESENT tHE FIVE BASIC FORCES of NATURE. KeepiNg These BaLaNCEd aNd uNder CONTROL is The Key To HaPPiNess!

KEEP YOUR CHI IN CHECK (CONT'd).

curves create good Chi ...

...bad Chi likes straight lines

PROBLEM

...STRESSED OUT?..

FENG SHUI SOLUTION

...bUiLd A PoNd...

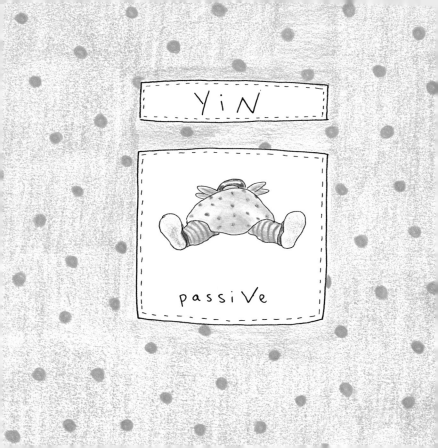

KEEP YOUR CHi iN CHECK (CONT'd)..

trees are good for Chi...

PROBLEM

...FEEL LIFELESS?..

FENG SHUI SOLUTION

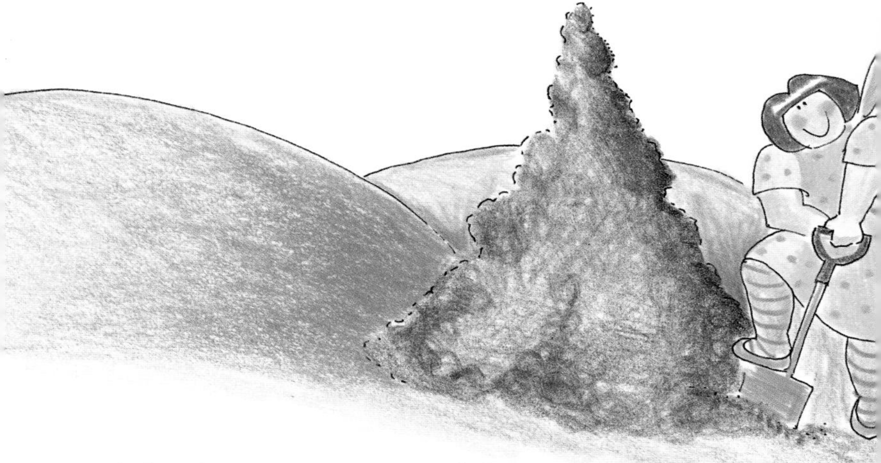

...CHANGE YOUR LANDSCAPE...

water soothes.........

. . . . a n d   c a l m s !

PROBLEM

...GOT NO MONEY?..

FENG SHUI SOLUTION

(tHe biGGeR, The BetteR!)

... GET A goLd BeLL...

KEEP YOUR CHi iN cHECK (CONT'd).

increasing your wealth Chi...

... brings rewards

ELEMENTAL !

FeNg SHui is bAsed upoN the
Five esSeNTiAl eLemeNTs.
EacH hAs PARTiCuLAr PropeRTies:

FiRe—FoR ExCiTeMeNT...

WATER — FOR CONTEMPLATION

WOOd — FOR EMOTIONAL GROWTH...

METAL — FOR POWER ...

EaRTh — foR stabiLity...

CHOCOLATE — FOR HAPPINESS*

*(THIS IS NOT STRICTLY ONE OF THE ELEMENTAL PILLARS OF "F.S." BUT IT BRINGS GREAT JOY IN MOST SITUATIONS!)

this is _very_ inauspicious!

water promotes good Chi...

YiN

sAd

PROBLEM

· · · · · · · · · · · · · · ·

...FEeL uNLUcKy?...

KEEP YOUR CHI IN CHECK (CONT'd).

bad Chi hangs around in corners...

ALTerNATiVely...

heDge youR BeTs aNd puT
Them aLL TogeTher !

KEEP YOUR CHi iN CHECK (CONTd).

bad Chi likes chipped crockery...

... so use the good stuff

a blast of loud music

...is an excellent tonic!...

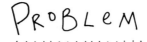

PROBLEM
....

...BAD MOOD?..

FENG SHUI SOLUTION

...WEAR A RED RIBBON...

KEEP YOUR CHI IN CHECK (CONT'D).

good Chi loves pets...

pets create

good energy !

KEEP YOUR CHI IN CHECK (CONT'd).

romantic Chi...

...likes things in pairs

...bored?..

FENG SHUI SOLUTION

...GEt A pET...

..........reorganizing your furniture...

...can affect your fate !!!..........

KEEP YOUR CHi iN CHECK (CONT'd).

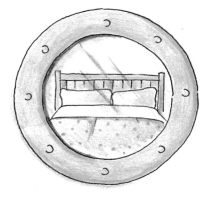

a mirror opposite your bed...

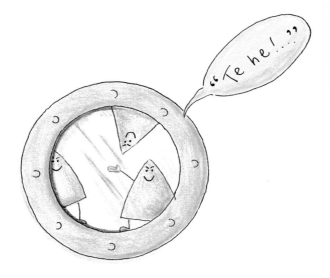

...attracts bad Chi...

.....plants in the home are soothing.........

..but prickly ones are trouble!.........

good Chi likes fresh flowers...

YIN

WEAK

PROBLEM

...FeeL eMpTy?..

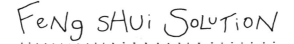

FENG SHUI SOLUTION

...KEEP YOUR REFRIGERATOR FULL...

...a t a n k f u l   of   g u p p i e s.........

Chi can expand...

... and contract

PROBLEM

...Unlucky in Love?..

FeNg sHUi SoLuTioN

...PUT two duCKs iN YOUR BedROOM...

crystals placed in your southwest corner . . . .

......can transform your social life!

KEEP YOUR CHi iN CHECK (CONT'd).

you can't see Chi...

...but it's <u>always</u> there...

... a firmly closed toilet lid.............

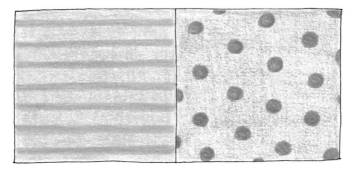

FLo's PERFECT HARMoNy!

REMEMBER...
FOR A BALANCED,
HAPPY LIFE
ALWAYS FOLLOW
YOUR INSTINCTS!

Lauren White spent much of her childhood at the bottom of the garden involved in a fruitless search for a real live fairy! Many years later, up popped Flo: Lauren comments "You imagine a shy, delicate creature with shimmering wings and a bell-like laugh—I got saddled with Flo!"

Flo has an opinion on everything. She's mischievous, subversive, and likes taking a very wry look at the antics of mortals. Lauren has managed to capture some of Flo's thoughts on aspects of the human condition and set them down in this little book.

Flo and Lauren live in the village of Cranfield in Bedfordshire, England, with Michael (mortal) and Jack (canine; terrified of Flo), where Lauren spends her spare time sketching, playing the piano, and adding to her collection of Victorian pixie lights (53 at present) by scouring antique shops and fairs. She has produced gift books celebrating life, books of spells (with Flo's guidance), and her designs for Hotchpotch greetings cards are sold around the world.

Sourcebooks, Inc.
P.O. Box 4410, Naperville, Illinois 60567-4410

(630) 961-3900
FAX: (630) 961-2168

Printed and bound in Spain

MQ 10 9 8 7 6 5 4 3 2 1

SBN: 1-57071-638-2